Cupc

C000225549

igloo

Published by Igloo Books Ltd
Cottage Farm
Sywell
NN6 0BJ
www.igloo-books.com

10 9 8 7 6 5 4 3 2 1

ISBN: 978 1 84852 730 0

Project Managed by R&R Publications Marketing Pty Ltd

Food Photography: R&R Photostudio (www.rrphotostudio.com.au)
Recipe Development: R&R Test Kitchen

Front cover photograph © Stockfood/L Ellert

Printed in and manufactured in China

Contents

Persian Vanilla

Preparation 12 mins **Cooking** 20 mins **Calories** 50

3 eggs
½ cup butter, softened
1 cup superfine sugar
½ cup milk
1½ cups self-rising flour, sifted
1 tsp vanilla extract

Topping
1 cup confectioner's sugar
1 tsp lemon extract
1 tsp vanilla extract
½ cup butter, room temperature
Candy floss

Note: Candy Floss (also known as Persian Fairy Floss) is available in specialist food stores.

1 Preheat the oven to 160°C (325°F). Line a 12-cupcake pan with cupcake papers. In a medium-sized bowl, lightly beat the eggs, add butter and sugar, then mix until light and fluffy.

2 Add milk, flour and vanilla, and stir to combine. Place in a blender and beat for 2 minutes, until light and creamy.

3 Divide the mixture evenly between the cake papers. Bake for 18–20 minutes until risen and firm to touch. Allow to cool for a few minutes and then transfer to a wire rack. Allow to cool fully before frosting.

Topping

1 Meanwhile, combine all topping ingredients except candy floss, mix with a wooden spoon until well combined, and beat with the spoon until light and fluffy.

2 Place mixture into a pastry bag with a star-shaped tip and pipe onto all cupcakes. Top with candy floss.

Makes 12

Vanilla Roses

Preparation 12 mins **Cooking** 20 mins **Calories** 46

3 eggs
½ cup butter, softened
1 cup superfine sugar
½ cup milk
1½ cups self-rising flour, sifted
1 tsp vanilla extract

Topping
1 cup confectioner's sugar
1 tsp rose water
½ cup butter, room temperature
6 drops vanilla extract
miniature dried roses, approximately 8 per cupcake (available from specialty cake decoration stores)

1 Preheat the oven to 160°C (325°F). Line a 12-cupcake pan with cupcake papers. In a medium-sized bowl, lightly beat the eggs, add butter and sugar, then mix until light and fluffy.

2 Add milk, flour and vanilla, and stir to combine. Place in a blender and beat for 2 minutes, until light and creamy.

3 Divide the mixture evenly between the cake papers. Bake for 18–20 minutes until risen and firm to touch. Allow to cool for a few minutes and then transfer to a wire rack. Allow to cool fully before frosting.

Topping

1 Meanwhile, combine half of all the topping ingredients except roses, mix with a wooden spoon, add remaining ingredients and beat with the spoon until light and fluffy. Place mixture into a pastry bag with a plain tip and pipe onto cupcakes. Decorate with roses.

Makes 12

Lavender Buttercream

Preparation 12 mins **Cooking** 20 mins **Calories** 45

3 eggs
½ cup butter, softened
1 cup superfine sugar
½ cup milk
1½ cups self-rising flour, sifted
1 tsp vanilla extract

Topping
1 cup confectioner's sugar
1 tsp lavender extract
½ cup butter, room temperature
2 drops purple food coloring
candied lavender (available from cake decoration stores)

1 Preheat the oven to 160°C (325°F). Line a 12-cupcake pan with cupcake papers. In a medium-sized bowl, lightly beat the eggs, add butter and sugar, then mix until light and fluffy.

2 Add milk, flour and vanilla, and stir to combine. Place in a blender and beat for 2 minutes, until light and creamy.

3 Divide the mixture evenly between the cake papers. Bake for 18–20 minutes until risen and firm to touch. Allow to cool for a few minutes and then transfer to a wire rack. Allow to cool fully before frosting.

Topping

1 Meanwhile, combine half the topping ingredients except candied lavender, mix with a wooden spoon, add remaining ingredients and beat with a whisk until light and fluffy.

2 Apply the topping with the back of a teaspoon or a small spatula. Place the candied lavender on top.

Makes 12

White Chocolate and Buttermilk

Preparation 12 mins **Cooking** 20 mins **Calories** 48

3 eggs
½ cup butter, softened
1 cup superfine sugar
½ cup buttermilk
1½ cups self-rising flour, sifted
1 tsp vanilla extract

Topping
100g (4oz) white chocolate, coarsely grated
1 tbsp butter
⅓ cup whipping cream
candied frangipanis (available from cake decoration stores)

1 Preheat the oven to 160°C (325°F). Line a 12-cupcake pan with cupcake papers. In a medium-sized bowl, lightly beat the eggs, add butter and sugar, then mix until light and fluffy.

2 Add buttermilk, flour and vanilla, and stir to combine. Place in a blender and beat for 2 minutes, until light and creamy.

3 Divide the mixture evenly between the cake papers. Bake for 18–20 minutes until risen and firm to touch. Allow to cool for a few minutes and then transfer to a wire rack. Allow to cool fully before frosting.

Topping

1 Meanwhile, combine the chocolate and butter in a medium-sized saucepan over a medium heat. As the mixture begins to melt, add the cream slowly, then reduce heat to low, stirring constantly, until mixture thickens.

2 Remove from heat and cool. Spread evenly onto cupcakes with a teaspoon and then top with frangipani decorations.

Makes 12

Marshmallow Vanilla Buttercups

Preparation 12 mins **Cooking** 20 mins **Calories** 43

3 eggs
½ cup butter, softened
1 cup superfine sugar
½ cup buttermilk
1½ cups self-rising flour, sifted
2 tsps vanilla extract

Topping
100g (4oz) confectioner's sugar
½ cup butter, room temperature
1 tsp vanilla extract
marshmallow dots (100g (4oz) minimum)

1 Preheat the oven to 160°C (325°F). Line a 12-cupcake pan with cupcake papers. In a medium-sized bowl, lightly beat the eggs, add butter and sugar, then mix until light and fluffy.

2 Add buttermilk, flour and vanilla, and stir to combine. Place in a blender and beat for 2 minutes, until light and creamy.

3 Divide the mixture evenly between the cake papers. Bake for 18–20 minutes until risen and firm to touch. Allow to cool for a few minutes and then transfer to a wire rack. Allow to cool fully before frosting.

Topping

1 Meanwhile, combine half the confectioner's sugar and butter, mix with a wooden spoon, add remaining confectioner's sugar, butter and vanilla extract and beat with the spoon until light and fluffy.

2 Add dollop (tablespoon-size) of topping to the center of each cake. Make a flower design with the small marshmallows in the center of each cupcake.

Makes 12

Double Whites

Preparation 12 mins **Cooking** 20 mins **Calories** 50

3 eggs
½ cup butter, softened
1 cup superfine sugar
½ cup milk
1½ cups self-rising flour, sifted
100g (4oz) white chocolate, grated
1 tsp vanilla extract

Topping
1 cup confectioner's sugar
½ cup butter, room temperature
72 silver balls
72 pre-made meringue decorations

1 Preheat the oven to 160°C (325°F). Line a 12-cupcake pan with cupcake papers. In a medium-sized bowl, lightly beat the eggs, add butter and sugar, then mix until light and fluffy.

2 Add the milk, flour, chocolate and vanilla, and stir to combine. Place in a blender and beat for 2 minutes, until light and creamy.

3 Divide the mixture evenly between the cake papers. Bake for 18–20 minutes until risen and firm to touch. Allow to cool for a few minutes and then transfer to a wire rack. Allow to cool fully before frosting.

Topping

1 Meanwhile, combine half the confectioner's sugar and butter, mix with a wooden spoon, add the remaining confectioner's sugar and butter and beat with the spoon until light and fluffy. Spoon onto cupcakes, leaving a little aside.

2 Using a dab of butter cream, place a silver ball at the center of each meringue, and then place them around each cupcake.

Makes 12

Triple Whites

Preparation 12 mins **Cooking** 20 mins **Calories** 56

3 eggs
½ cup butter, softened
1 cup superfine sugar
½ cup milk
1½ cups self-rising flour, sifted
1 tsp vanilla extract
100g (4oz) white chocolate, chopped

Topping
200g (8oz) white chocolate buttons
1 tbsp butter
⅓ cup whipping cream,
½ cup butter, room temperature
½ cup confectioner's sugar

1 Preheat the oven to 160°C (325°F). Line a 12-cupcake pan with cupcake papers. In a medium-sized bowl, lightly beat the eggs, add butter and sugar, then mix until light and fluffy.

2 Add milk, flour and vanilla, and stir to combine. Place in a blender and beat for 2 minutes, until light and creamy. Add white chocolate and stir through the mixture.

3 Divide the mixture evenly between the cake papers. Bake for 18–20 minutes until risen and firm to touch. Allow to cool for a few minutes and then transfer to a wire rack. Allow to cool fully before frosting.

Topping

1 Meanwhile, combine 160g (5oz) of the white chocolate with 1 tablespoon of butter in a medium-sized saucepan over a medium heat. As the mixture begins to melt, add the cream slowly, then reduce heat to low, stirring constantly, until mixture thickens. Remove from heat and cool.

2 Combine butter and confectioner's sugar, and mix with a wooden spoon. Beat with the spoon until light and fluffy. Add melted chocolate, combine, then spoon onto cupcakes. Top with remaining white chocolate buttons.

Makes 12

Vanilla Hearts

Preparation 12 mins **Cooking** 20 mins **Calories** 26

3 eggs
½ cup butter, softened
1 cup superfine sugar
½ cup milk
1½ cups self-rising flour, sifted
1 tsp vanilla extract
100g (4oz) white chocolate, chopped

Topping
⅓ cup confectioner's sugar
2 tbsps water
⅓ cup seedless strawberry preserve
heart-shaped candles

1 Preheat the oven to 160°C (325°F). Line a 12-cupcake pan with cupcake papers. In a medium-sized bowl, lightly beat the eggs, add butter and sugar, then mix until light and fluffy.

1 Add milk, flour and vanilla, and stir to combine. Place in a blender and beat for 2 minutes, until light and creamy. Add white chocolate and stir through the mixture.

1 Divide the mixture evenly between the cake papers. Bake for 18–20 minutes until risen and firm to touch. Allow to cool for a few minutes and then transfer to a wire rack. Allow to cool fully before frosting.

Topping

1 Meanwhile, combine confectioner's sugar and water in a small bowl. Add strawberry preserve to a pastry bag using the smallest pastry tip, and pipe over the cake. Repeat with white frosting. Top with heart-shaped candle.

Makes 12

Vanilla Sprinkles

Preparation 12 mins **Cooking** 20 mins **Calories** 40

3 eggs
½ cup butter, softened
1 cup superfine sugar
½ cup milk
1½ cups self-rising flour, sifted
1 tsp vanilla extract
1 tsp cocoa powder

Topping
½ cup confectioner's sugar
¾ tbsp hot water
sprinkles (or 100s & 1000s)

1 Preheat the oven to 160°C (325°F). Line a 12-cupcake pan with cupcake papers. In a medium-sized bowl, lightly beat the eggs, add butter and sugar, then mix until light and fluffy.

2 Add milk, flour and vanilla, and stir to combine. Place in a blender and beat for 2 minutes, until light and creamy.

3 Divide the mixture in half, and add the vanilla to one half and cocoa powder to the other, and divide evenly between the cake papers. Bake for 18–20 minutes until risen and firm to touch. Allow to cool for a few minutes and then transfer to a wire rack. Allow to cool fully before frosting.

Topping

1 Meanwhile, combine confectioner's sugar and water in a small bowl, and mix with a wooden spoon. Spoon onto cupcakes. Tip sprinkles onto a small plate and gently press each cupcake into the sprinkles.

Makes 12

Butterfly Cakes

Preparation 12 mins **Cooking** 20 mins **Calories** 41

3 eggs
½ cup butter, softened
1 cup superfine sugar
½ cup milk
1½ cups self-rising flour, sifted
1 tsp vanilla extract

Topping
1 cup confectioner's sugar
1 tsp vanilla extract
½ cup butter, room temperature

Variation: Use 1½ cups of whipping cream and 2 tbsps preserve as the topping. Divide the cream and preserve between the cupcakes.

1 Preheat the oven to 160°C (325°F). Line a 12-cupcake pan with cupcake papers. In a medium-sized bowl, lightly beat the eggs, add butter and sugar, then mix until light and fluffy.

2 Add milk, flour and vanilla, and stir to combine. Place in a blender and beat for 2 minutes, until light and creamy.

3 Divide the mixture evenly between the cake papers. Bake for 18–20 minutes until risen and firm to touch. Allow to cool for a few minutes and then transfer to a wire rack. Allow to cool fully before frosting.

Topping

1 Meanwhile, combine all topping ingredients, mix with a wooden spoon until well combined, then beat with the spoon until light and fluffy.

2 Place mixture into a pastry bag, and set aside. Using a sharp knife, cut a 10cm (4in) circle into the center of each cupcake, slicing the top off. Cut these circles in half and set aside. Fill the center of each cupcake with frosting, and stand the two pieces of cake top upright, to form wings.

Makes 12

Butter Choc

Preparation 12 mins **Cooking** 20 mins **Calories** 42

3 eggs
½ cup butter, softened
1 cup superfine sugar
½ cup buttermilk
1½ cups self-rising flour, sifted
1 tsp cocoa powder
1 tsp vanilla extract
½ cup milk chocolate pieces,
finely chopped
⅓ cup whipping cream

Topping

1 cup confectioner's sugar
½ cup butter, room
temperature
5 drops pink food coloring
sugar flowers (available from
cake decoration shops)

1 Preheat the oven to 160°C (325°F). Line a 12-cupcake pan with cupcake papers. In a medium-sized bowl, lightly beat the eggs, add butter and sugar, then mix until light and fluffy.

2 Add buttermilk, flour, cocoa powder and vanilla, and stir to combine. Place in a blender and beat for 2 minutes, until light and creamy. Add milk chocolate and stir through mixture.

3 Divide the mixture evenly between the cake papers. Bake for 18–20 minutes until risen and firm to touch. Allow to cool for a few minutes and then transfer to a wire rack. Allow to cool fully before frosting.

Topping

1 Meanwhile, combine half the confectioner's sugar and butter, mix with a wooden spoon, add remaining confectioner's sugar, butter and food coloring and beat with the spoon until light and fluffy. Add frosting to a pastry bag and pipe onto cupcakes, then smooth over with spatula and top with flower decorations.

Makes 12

Orange Ganache

Preparation 12 mins **Cooking** 20 mins **Calories** 41

3 eggs
½ cup butter, softened
1 cup superfine sugar
½ cup milk
1½ cups self-rising flour, sifted
1 tsp vanilla extract
100g (4oz) bittersweet chocolate pieces
1 tbsp cocoa powder
1 tsp orange extract

Topping
100g (4oz) bittersweet chocolate, grated
20g (1oz) butter
⅓ cup whipping cream
1 tsp orange extract
1 piece candied orange, cut into slivers

1 Preheat the oven to 160°C (325°F). Line a 12-cupcake pan with cupcake papers. In a medium-sized bowl, lightly beat the eggs, add butter and sugar, then mix until light and fluffy.

2 Add milk, flour and vanilla, and stir to combine. Add remaining ingredients. Place in a blender and beat for 2 minutes, until light and creamy.

3 Divide the mixture evenly between the cake papers. Bake for 18–20 minutes until risen and firm to touch. Allow to cool for a few minutes and then transfer to a wire rack. Allow to cool fully before frosting.

Topping

1 Meanwhile, combine the chocolate and butter in a medium-sized saucepan over a medium heat. As the mixture begins to melt, reduce heat to low, stirring constantly, until melted. Remove from heat, add cream, orange extract, and stir. Rest for 10 minutes: the mixture will be firm and velvety in consistency. Once cool, put in a pastry bag with a small plain tip.

2 Pipe topping onto cupcakes in a spiral and top with candied orange pieces.

Makes 12

Persian Chocolate

Preparation 12 mins **Cooking** 20 mins **Calories** 42

3 eggs
½ cup butter, softened
1 cup superfine sugar
½ cup milk
1½ cups self-rising flour, sifted
1 tsp vanilla extract
100g (4oz) bittersweet chocolate pieces
1 tbsp cocoa powder

Topping

1 cup confectioner's sugar
½ cup butter, room temperature
2 tsps cocoa powder
small packet of candy floss (see p.4)
1 tbsp cocoa powder, for dusting

1 Preheat the oven to 160°C (325°F). Line a 12-cupcake pan with cupcake papers. In a medium-sized bowl, lightly beat the eggs, add butter and sugar, then mix until light and fluffy.

2 Add milk, flour and vanilla, and stir to combine. Add remaining ingredients. Place in a blender and beat for 2 minutes, until light and creamy.

3 Divide the mixture evenly between the cake papers. Bake for 18–20 minutes until risen and firm to touch. Allow to cool for a few minutes and then transfer to a wire rack. Allow to cool fully before frosting.

Topping

1 Meanwhile, combine half the confectioner's sugar and butter, mix with a wooden spoon, add remaining confectioner's sugar, butter and cocoa powder and beat with the spoon until light and fluffy.

2 Add frosting to a pastry bag with a small tip and pipe onto cupcakes in a spiral. Top with candy floss and a dusting of cocoa.

Makes 12

Vanilla Choc

Preparation 12 mins **Cooking** 20 mins **Calories** 38g

3 eggs
½ cup butter, softened
1 cup superfine sugar
½ cup vanilla-flavored yogurt
1½ cups self-rising flour, sifted
1 tbsp vanilla extract
100g (4oz) bittersweet chocolate pieces
1 tbsp cocoa

Topping
100g (4oz) bittersweet chocolate pieces
20g (1oz) butter
⅓ cup whipping cream,
silver balls (available from cake decoration stores)

1 Preheat the oven to 160°C (325°F). Line a 12-cupcake pan with cupcake papers. In a medium-sized bowl, lightly beat the eggs, add butter and sugar, then mix until light and fluffy.

2 Add milk, flour and vanilla, and stir to combine. Add remaining ingredients. Place in a blender and beat for 2 minutes, until light and creamy.

3 Divide the mixture evenly between the cake papers. Bake for 18–20 minutes until risen and firm to touch. Allow to cool for a few minutes, and then transfer to a wire rack. Allow to cool fully before frosting.

Topping

1 Meanwhile, combine the chocolate and butter in a medium-sized saucepan over a medium heat. As the mixture begins to melt, reduce heat to low, stirring constantly, until melted. Remove from heat, add cream, and stir. Rest for 10 minutes: the mixture will be firm and velvety in consistency. Use a fork to apply frosting to each cupcake, and add silver balls to finish.

Makes 12

Hazel Choc

Preparation 12 mins **Cooking** 20 mins **Calories** 55

3 eggs
½ cup butter, softened
1 cup superfine sugar
½ cup milk
1½ cups self-rising flour, sifted
1 tsp vanilla extract
100g (4oz) bittersweet chocolate pieces
1 tbsp cocoa powder

Topping
100g (4oz) bittersweet chocolate pieces
1 tbsp butter
⅓ cup whipping cream
½ cup butter, room temperature
½ cup confectioner's sugar
100g (4oz) hazelnuts

1 Preheat the oven to 160°C (325°F). Line a 12-cupcake pan with cupcake papers. In a medium-sized bowl, lightly beat the eggs, add butter and sugar, then mix until light and fluffy.

2 Add milk, flour and vanilla, and stir to combine. Add remaining ingredients. Place in a blender and beat for 2 minutes, until light and creamy.

3 Divide the mixture evenly between the cake papers. Bake for 18–20 minutes until risen and firm to touch. Allow to cool for a few minutes and then transfer to a wire rack. Allow to cool fully before frosting.

Topping

1 Meanwhile, combine the chocolate and 1 tablespoon of butter in a medium-sized saucepan over a medium heat. As the mixture begins to melt, add cream slowly, then reduce heat to low, stirring constantly, until mixture thickens. Remove from heat and cool.

2 Combine butter and confectioner's sugar, and mix with wooden spoon. Beat with the spoon until light and fluffy. Add melted chocolate and ½ of the hazelnuts, combine, and then spoon onto cupcakes. Top with the remaining nuts.

Makes 12

Chili Choc

Preparation 12 mins **Cooking** 20 mins **Calories** 41

2 small fresh chilies or 1 tsp
dry red chili flakes

3 eggs

½ cup butter, softened

1 cup superfine sugar

½ cup milk

1½ cups self-rising flour, sifted

1 tsp vanilla extract

100g (4oz) bittersweet
chocolate pieces

1 tbsp cocoa powder

Topping

100g (4oz) bittersweet
chocolate, chopped

20g (1oz) butter

⅓ cup whipping cream

remaining chili-infused water

chilies for decoration

1 Preheat the oven to 160°C (325°F). Line a 12-cupcake pan with cupcake papers. Slice chilies down the center and remove seeds. Place the chilies in a cup with ¼ cup of hot water to soak for 10 minutes. In a medium-sized bowl, lightly beat the eggs, add butter and sugar, then mix until light and fluffy.

2 Add milk, flour and vanilla, and stir to combine. Add ½ cup bittersweet chocolate, cocoa powder and half the chili-infused water and combine. Place in a blender and beat for 2 minutes, until light and creamy.

3 Divide the mixture evenly between the cake papers. Bake for 18–20 minutes until risen and firm to touch. Allow to cool for a few minutes and then transfer to a wire rack. Allow to cool fully before frosting.

Topping

1 Meanwhile, combine the chocolate and butter in a medium-sized saucepan over a medium heat. As the mixture begins to melt, reduce heat to low, stirring constantly, until melted. Remove from heat, add cream, remaining chili water and stir. Rest for 10 minutes: the mixture will be firm and velvety in consistency. Put in a pastry bag with a small plain tip and pipe onto cakes. Top with fresh small chilies.

Makes 12

Triple Choc

Preparation 12 mins **Cooking** 20 mins **Calories** 40

3 eggs
½ cup butter, softened
1 cup superfine sugar
½ cup milk
1½ cups self-rising flour, sifted
100g (4oz) bittersweet chocolate pieces
1 tbsp cocoa powder

Topping
100g (4oz) bittersweet chocolate, chopped
20g (1oz) butter
⅓ cup whipping cream
2 tbsps cocoa powder
1 tsp confectioner's sugar

1 Preheat the oven to 160°C (325°F). Line a 12-cupcake pan with cupcake papers. In a medium-sized bowl, lightly beat the eggs, add butter and sugar, then mix until light and fluffy.

2 Add milk and flour, and stir to combine. Add ½ cup bittersweet chocolate and cocoa powder, and stir through mixture. Place in a blender and beat for 2 minutes, until light and creamy.

3 Divide the mixture evenly between the cupcake papers. Bake for 18–20 minutes until risen and firm to touch. Allow to cool for a few minutes and then transfer to a wire rack. Allow to cool fully before frosting.

Topping

1 Meanwhile, combine the chocolate and butter in a medium-sized saucepan over a medium heat. As the mixture begins to melt, reduce heat to low, stirring constantly, until melted. Remove from heat, add cream, cocoa powder and confectioner's sugar, and stir to combine. Rest for 10 minutes: the mixture will be firm and velvety in consistency. Use the back of a spoon to apply frosting to cupcake.

Makes 12

Choc Chip

Preparation 12 mins **Cooking** 20 mins **Calories** 644 **Fat** 46g

3 eggs
½ cup butter, softened
1 cup superfine sugar
½ cup milk
1½ cups self-rising flour, sifted
1 tsp vanilla extract
120g (4½oz) milk chocolate drops
1 tbsp cocoa powder

Topping
½ cup milk chocolate, grated
1 cup butter, room temperature
⅓ cup whipping cream
1 cup confectioner's sugar
1 tsp vanilla extract
½ cup milk chocolate drops
½ cup small choc drops

Variation: You could add 1 tsp instant coffee to the cupcake mix and 1 tsp of instant coffee to the topping mix to make a mocha choc chip cupcake.

1 Preheat the oven to 160°C (325°F). Line a 12-cupcake pan with cupcake papers. In a medium-sized bowl, lightly beat the eggs, add butter and sugar, then mix until light and fluffy.

2 Place in a blender and beat for 2 minutes, until light and creamy. Add milk, flour and vanilla, and stir to combine. Add ½ cup milk chocolate and cocoa powder, and stir through mixture.

3 Divide the mixture evenly between the cupcake papers. Bake for 18–20 minutes until risen and firm to touch. Allow to cool for a few minutes and then transfer to a wire rack. Allow to cool fully before frosting.

Topping

1 Meanwhile, combine the chocolate and half the butter in a medium-sized saucepan over a medium heat. As the mixture begins to melt, reduce heat to low, stirring constantly, until melted. Remove from heat, add cream, and stir. Rest for 10 minutes: the mixture will be firm and velvety in consistency.

2 Combine remaining butter, confectioner's sugar and vanilla extract, stir until light and fluffy. Add melted chocolate mixture, stir in chocolate drops and spoon onto cupcakes. Sprinkle with small chocolate drops.

Makes 12

Chocolate Sponge Toffee

Preparation 12 mins **Cooking** 20 mins **Calories** 60

3 eggs
½ cup butter, softened
1 cup superfine sugar
½ cup buttermilk
1½ cups self-rising flour, sifted
1 tsp vanilla extract

Topping
½ cup chocolate drops
½ cup butter, room temperature
⅓ cup whipping cream
1 cup confectioner's sugar
1 tsp vanilla extract
½ cup pre-made sponge toffee pieces

Variation: Instead of using the sponge toffee pieces, you could break 2 peppermint chocolate bars and top each cake with a cluster of the crumbled peppermint chocolate

1 Preheat the oven to 160°C (325°F). Line a 12-cupcake pan with cupcake papers. In a medium-sized bowl, lightly beat the eggs, add butter and sugar, then mix until light and fluffy.

2 Add buttermilk, flour and vanilla, and stir to combine. Place in a blender and beat for 2 minutes, until light and creamy.

3 Divide the mixture evenly between the cupcake papers. Bake for 18–20 minutes until risen and firm to touch. Allow to cool for a few minutes and then transfer to a wire rack. Allow to cool fully before frosting.

Topping

1 Meanwhile, combine the chocolate and half the butter in a medium-sized saucepan over a medium heat. As the mixture begins to melt, reduce heat to low, stirring constantly, until melted. Remove from heat, add cream, and stir. Rest for 10 minutes, the mixture will be firm and velvety in consistency.

2 Combine remaining butter, confectioner's sugar and vanilla extract, and stir until light and fluffy. Add melted chocolate mixture, and stir to combine. Apply frosting to each cupcake with a knife. Top each cupcake with a cluster of crumbled sponge toffee.

Makes 12

Chocky Road

Preparation 12 mins **Cooking** 20 mins **Calories** 59

3 eggs
½ cup butter, softened
1 cup superfine sugar
½ cup milk
1½ cups self-rising flour, sifted
1 tsp vanilla extract
1 tbsp cocoa powder

Topping
½ cup milk chocolate drops
½ cup butter, room temperature
⅓ cup whipping cream
1 cup confectioner's sugar
1 tsp vanilla extract
¼ cup candied cherries, chopped
⅓ cup almonds, chopped
⅓ cup marshmallows, chopped

1 Preheat the oven to 160°C (325°F). Line a 12-cupcake pan with cupcake papers. In a medium-sized bowl, lightly beat the eggs, add butter and sugar, then mix until light and fluffy.

2 Add milk, flour, vanilla and cocoa powder, and stir to combine. Place in a blender and beat for 2 minutes, until light and creamy.

3 Divide the mixture evenly between the cupcake papers. Bake for 18–20 minutes until risen and firm to touch. Allow to cool for a few minutes and then transfer to a wire rack. Allow to cool fully before frosting.

Topping

1 Meanwhile, combine the chocolate and half the butter in a medium-sized saucepan over a medium heat. As the mixture begins to melt, reduce heat to low, stirring constantly, until melted. Remove from heat, add cream, and stir. Rest for 10 minutes: the mixture will be firm and velvety in consistency.

2 Combine remaining butter, confectioner's sugar and vanilla extract, and stir until light and fluffy. Add melted chocolate mixture and stir to combine. Ice the top of each cupcake and decorate with pieces of cherry, almonds and marshmallows.

Makes 12

Almond Choc

Preparation 12 mins **Cooking** 45 mins **Calories** 64

3 eggs
½ cup butter, softened
1 cup superfine sugar
½ cup milk
1½ cups self-rising flour, sifted
1 tsp vanilla extract
1 tbsp cocoa powder

Topping

½ cup superfine sugar, for toffee
100g (4oz) bittersweet chocolate
20g (1oz) butter
⅓ cup whipping cream
1 cup confectioner's sugar
1 tbsp cocoa powder
½ cup bittersweet chocolate
100g (4oz) slivered almonds

1 Preheat the oven to 160°C (325°F). Line a 12-cupcake pan with cupcake papers. In a medium-sized bowl, lightly beat the eggs, add butter and sugar, then mix until light and fluffy.

2 Add milk, flour, vanilla and cocoa powder, and stir to combine. Place in a blender and beat for 2 minutes, until light and creamy.

3 Divide the mixture evenly between the cupcake papers. Bake for 18–20 minutes until risen and firm to touch. Allow to cool for a few minutes and then transfer to a wire rack. Allow to cool fully before frosting.

Toffee

1 Place ½ cup superfine sugar evenly on a cooking parchment-lined baking tray, and bake in oven on 200°C (400°F) for approximately 25 minutes until toffee consistency forms. Cool until hardened.

Topping

1 Combine the chocolate and butter in a medium-sized saucepan over a medium heat. As the mixture begins to melt, reduce heat to low, stirring constantly, until melted. Remove from heat, add cream, and stir. Rest for 10 minutes: the mixture will be firm and velvety in consistency.

2 Combine the confectioner's sugar and cocoa powder, mix with wooden spoon until mixed together, beat with spoon until light and fluffy. Add the chocolate mixture to the butter cream and mix with a wooden spoon until light and fluffy. Ice the cakes. Decorate with slivered almonds and broken toffee pieces.

Makes 12

Cherry Choc

Preparation 12 mins **Cooking** 20 mins **Calories** 58

3 eggs
½ cup butter, softened
1 cup confectioner's sugar
½ cup milk
1 tbsp kirsch liqueur
1½ cups self-rising flour, sifted
200g (8oz) white chocolate, chopped

Topping
100g (4oz) white chocolate, chopped
1 tbsp butter
⅓ cup whipping cream,
1 tbsp cherry liqueur
⅔ cup confectioner's sugar
½ cup butter, room temperature
200g (8oz) candied cherries, chopped

1 Preheat the oven to 160°C (325°F). Line a 12-cupcake pan with cupcake papers. In a medium-sized bowl, lightly beat the eggs, add butter and sugar, then mix until light and fluffy.

2 Add milk, liqueur and flour, and stir to combine. Place in a blender and beat for 2 minutes, until light and creamy. Add white chocolate, and stir through mixture.

3 Divide the mixture evenly between the cake papers. Bake for 18–20 minutes until risen and firm to touch. Allow to cool for a few minutes and then transfer to a wire rack. Allow to cool fully before frosting.

Topping

1 Meanwhile, combine the chocolate and tablespoon of butter in a medium-sized saucepan over a medium heat. As the mixture begins to melt, add cream and liqueur slowly, then reduce heat to low, stirring constantly until mixture thickens. Remove from heat and cool.

2 Combine butter and confectioner's sugar, and mix with a wooden spoon. Beat with the spoon until light and fluffy. Add melted chocolate and candied cherries, stir until combined, and then spoon onto cupcakes.

Makes 12

Triple Berry

Preparation 12 mins   **Cooking** 20 mins   **Calories** 27

3 eggs
½ cup butter, softened
1 cup superfine sugar
½ cup milk
2 tbsps raspberry liqueur
1½ cups self-rising flour, sifted

Topping
½ cup confectioner's sugar
2 tbsps water
200g (8oz) strawberries
200g (8oz) blueberries
200g (8oz) blackberries

*Variation: Add ¼ cup mixed
crushed berries to the cupcake
mix before baking.*

1 Preheat the oven to 160°C (325°F). Line a 12-cupcake pan with cupcake papers. In a medium-sized bowl, lightly beat the eggs, add butter and sugar, then mix until light and fluffy.

2 Add milk, liqueur and flour, and stir to combine. Place in a blender and beat for 2 minutes, until light and creamy.

3 Divide the mixture evenly between the cake papers. Bake for 18–20 minutes until risen and firm to touch. Allow to cool for a few minutes and then transfer to a wire rack. Allow to cool fully before frosting.

Topping

1 Meanwhile, combine confectioner's sugar and water in a small bowl. Spoon a teaspoon of frosting in the center of each cupcake. Decorate with a cluster of fresh berries.

Makes 12

Passion Yogurt

Preparation 12 mins **Cooking** 20 mins **Calories** 35

3 eggs
½ cup butter, softened
1 cup superfine sugar
½ cup plain yogurt
1½ cups self-rising flour, sifted
1 tsp vanilla extract
the pulp of 2 passion fruit

Topping
1 cup confectioner's sugar
½ cup of Greek-style yogurt
the pulp of 1 passion fruit

1 Preheat the oven to 160°C (325°F). Line a 12 cupcake pan with cupcake papers. In a medium-sized bowl, lightly beat the eggs, add butter and sugar, then mix until light and fluffy.

2 Add yogurt, flour and vanilla, and stir to combine. Place in a blender and beat for 2 minutes, until light and creamy. Fold passion fruit pulp through mixture.

3 Divide the mixture evenly between the cake papers. Bake for 18–20 minutes until risen and firm to touch. Allow to cool for a few minutes and then transfer to a wire rack. Allow to cool fully before frosting.

Topping

1 Meanwhile, combine confectioner's sugar and yogurt in a medium-sized bowl and mix with a wooden spoon. Add passion fruit pulp, mix to combine and spread topping on cupcakes.

Makes 12

Black Forest

Preparation 12 mins **Cooking** 20 mins **Calories** 29

3 eggs
½ cup butter, softened
1 cup superfine sugar
½ cup milk
1½ cups self-rising flour, sifted
1 tbsp kirsch liqueur
¼ cup cocoa powder

Topping
100g (4oz) whipping cream
12 fresh cherries
¼ cup chocolate, shaved

1 Preheat the oven to 160°C (325°F). Line a 12-cupcake pan with cupcake papers. In a medium-sized bowl, lightly beat the eggs, add butter and sugar, then mix until light and fluffy.

2 Add milk, flour and cocoa powder, and stir to combine. Place in a blender and beat for 2 minutes, until light and creamy, then fold through kirsch liqueur.

3 Divide the mixture evenly between the cake papers. Bake for 18–20 minutes until risen and firm to touch. Allow to cool for a few minutes and then transfer to a wire rack. Allow to cool fully before frosting.

Topping

1 Meanwhile, beat cream until stiff peaks form, then top each cake with a spoonful of cream, a sprinkle of chocolate shavings and a fresh cherry.

Makes 12

Poppy Lime

Preparation 12 mins **Cooking** 20 mins **Calories** 41

3 eggs
½ cup butter, softened
1 cup superfine sugar
½ cup Greek-style yogurt
1½ cups self-rising flour, sifted
zest of 2 limes
juice of 1 lime
1 tsp poppy seeds

Topping
1 cup confectioner's sugar
½ cup butter, room temperature
juice of 1 lime
½ tsp poppy seeds
zest of 1 lime
50g (2oz) candied lime, cut into thin slivers

1 Preheat the oven to 160°C (325°F). Line a 12-cupcake pan with cupcake papers. In a medium-sized bowl, lightly beat the eggs, add butter and sugar, then mix until light and fluffy.

1 Add yogurt and flour, and stir to combine. Place in a blender and beat for 2 minutes, until light and creamy. Add lime zest, lime juice and poppy seeds, and mix through with a wooden spoon.

1 Divide the mixture evenly between the cake cases. Bake for 18–20 minutes until risen and firm to touch. Allow to cool for a few minutes and then transfer to a wire rack. Allow to cool fully before frosting.

Topping

1 Meanwhile, combine the topping ingredients, mix with a wooden spoon, and spoon onto cakes. Top with candied lime pieces.

Makes 12

Apple and Cinnamon

Preparation 12 mins **Cooking** 20 mins **Calories** 41

½ apple, peeled and chopped into small pieces

juice of 1 lemon

1 tbsp cinnamon

3 eggs

½ cup butter, softened

1 cup superfine sugar

½ cup milk

1½ cups self-rising flour, sifted

Topping

1 cup confectioner's sugar

½ cup butter, room temperature

1 tbsp cinnamon sugar

1 Preheat the oven to 160°C (325°F). Line a 12-cupcake pan with cupcake papers. In a small bowl, coat the apple pieces with lemon juice and sprinkle with cinnamon. In a medium-sized bowl, lightly beat the eggs, add butter and sugar, then mix until light and fluffy.

2 Add milk and flour, and stir to combine. Place in a blender and beat for 2 minutes, until light and creamy. Add spiced apple and stir through mixture.

3 Divide the mixture evenly between the cake papers. Bake for 18–20 minutes until risen and firm to touch. Allow to cool for a few minutes and then transfer to a wire rack. Allow to cool fully before frosting.

Topping

1 Meanwhile, combine half the confectioner's sugar and butter, mix with a wooden spoon, add remaining confectioner's sugar and butter and beat with the spoon until light and fluffy. Spoon topping onto cupcakes and sprinkle cinnamon sugar on top.

Makes 12

Orange Poppy

Preparation 12 mins **Cooking** 20 mins **Calories** 42

3 eggs
½ cup butter, softened
1 cup superfine sugar
½ cup buttermilk
1½ cups self-rising flour, sifted
zest of 1 orange
juice of ½ orange
1 tsp poppy seeds

Topping

1 cup confectioner's sugar
½ cup butter, room temperature
juice of ½ orange
½ tesp poppy seeds
zest of 1 orange
candied orange pieces, cut into thin slivers

1 Preheat the oven to 160°C (325°F). Line a 12-cupcake pan with cupcake papers. In a medium-sized bowl, lightly beat the eggs, add butter and sugar, then mix until light and fluffy.

2 Add buttermilk and flour, and stir to combine. Place in a blender and beat for 2 minutes, until light and creamy. Add orange zest, orange juice and poppy seeds, and mix through with a wooden spoon.

3 Divide the mixture evenly between the cake cases. Bake for 18–20 minutes until risen and firm to touch. Allow to cool for a few minutes and then transfer to a wire rack. Allow to cool fully before frosting.

Topping

1 Meanwhile, combine topping ingredients, and mix with a wooden spoon. Spoon onto cakes. Top with candied orange pieces.

Makes 12

Variation: Add lime juice and rind instead of orange.

Blue Bells

Preparation 12 mins **Cooking** 20 mins **Calories** 27

3 eggs
½ cup butter, softened
1 cup superfine sugar
½ cup milk
1½ cups self-rising flour, sifted
1 tsp vanilla extract
200g (8oz) blueberries, chopped in half

Topping
1 cup confectioner's sugar
2 tbsps of blueberries, mashed
½ punnet blueberries

1 Preheat the oven to 160°C (325°F). Line a 12-cupcake pan with cupcake papers. In a medium-sized bowl, lightly beat the eggs, add butter and sugar, then mix until light and fluffy.

2 Add milk, flour and vanilla, and stir to combine. Place in a blender and beat for 2 minutes, until light and creamy. Add blueberries and stir through the mixture.

3 Divide the mixture evenly between the cake papers. Bake for 18–20 minutes until risen and firm to touch. Allow to cool for a few minutes and then transfer to a wire rack. Allow to cool fully before frosting.

Topping

1 Meanwhile, combine confectioner's sugar and mashed berries in a medium-sized bowl and mix with wooden spoon. Use a spatula to apply frosting to each cupcake and top with a blueberry.

Makes 12

Banana Nut

Preparation 12 mins **Cooking** 20 mins **Calories** 44

3 eggs
½ cup butter, softened
1 cup superfine sugar
½ cup milk
1½ cups self-rising flour, sifted
1 tsp smooth peanut butter
1 banana, mashed

Topping
½ cup superfine sugar, for toffee
1 cup confectioner's sugar
½ cup butter, room temperature
2 tbsps crunchy unsalted peanut butter
1 tbsp corn syrup

1 Preheat the oven to 160°C (325°F). Line a 12-cupcake pan with cupcake papers. In a medium-sized bowl, lightly beat the eggs, add butter and sugar, then mix until light and fluffy.

2 Add milk, flour, peanut butter and banana, and stir to combine. Place in a blender and beat for 2 minutes, until light and creamy. Add banana and stir through mix.

3 Divide the mixture evenly between the cake papers. Bake for 18–20 minutes until risen and firm to touch. Allow to cool for a few minutes and then transfer to a wire rack. Allow to cool fully before frosting.

Toffee

1 Place ½ cup superfine sugar evenly on a cooking parchment-lined baking tray, and bake in oven on 200°C (400°F) for approximately 25 minutes until toffee consistency forms. Cool until hardened.

Topping

1 Meanwhile, combine half the confectioner's sugar, butter and peanut butter, and mix with a wooden spoon, then add remaining confectioner's sugar, butter and peanut butter and beat with the spoon until light and fluffy. Use the back of a spoon to frost cakes. Drizzle corn syrup onto cakes and top with toffee pieces.

Makes 12

Peachy Pieces

Preparation 12 mins   **Cooking** 20 mins   **Calories** 42

3 eggs
½ cup butter, softened
1 cup superfine sugar
½ cup milk
1½ cups self-rising flour, sifted
2 tbsps peach liqueur

Topping
1 cup confectioner's sugar
½ cup butter, room temperature
1 tsp peach extract
1 drop orange food coloring
1 drop red food coloring
peach-colored sugar flowers (available from cake decoration stores)

1   Preheat the oven to 160°C (325°F). Line a 12-cupcake pan with cupcake papers. In a medium-sized bowl, lightly beat the eggs, add butter and sugar, then mix until light and fluffy.

2   Add milk, flour and peach liqueur, stir to combine. Place in a blender and beat for 2 minutes, until light and creamy.

3   Divide the mixture evenly between the cake cases. Bake for 18–20 minutes until risen and firm to touch. Allow to cool for a few minutes and then transfer to a wire rack. Allow to cool fully before frosting.

Topping

1   Meanwhile, combine all topping ingredients except the sugar flower in a small bowl. Mix with a wooden spoon, then beat with a whisk until light and fluffy. Spoon mixture into a pastry bag and pipe dots onto all cupcakes. Top each dot of frosting with a flower.

Makes 12

Strawberry Surprise

Preparation 12 mins **Cooking** 20 mins **Calories** 43

3 eggs
½ cup butter, softened
1 cup superfine sugar
½ cup milk
1½ cups self-rising flour, sifted
2 tbsps strawberry liqueur

Topping
1 cup confectioner's sugar
½ cup butter, room temperature
3 strawberries, quartered
strawberry-colored flowers (available from cake decoration stores)

Variation: Use raspberries and raspberry liqueur instead of strawberries.

1 Preheat the oven to 160°C (325°F). Line a 12-cupcake pan, with cupcake papers. In a medium-sized bowl, lightly beat the eggs, add butter and sugar, then mix until light and fluffy.

2 Add milk, flour and liqueur, and stir to combine. Place in a blender and beat for 2 minutes, until light and creamy.

3 Divide the mixture evenly between the cake papers. Bake for 18–20 minutes until risen and firm to touch. Allow to cool for a few minutes and then transfer to a wire rack. Allow to cool fully before frosting.

Topping

1 Meanwhile, combine confectioner's sugar and butter in a small bowl, mix with a wooden spoon until well combined, then beat with a whisk until light and fluffy. Spoon mixture into a pastry bag with a medium-sized star-shaped tip, and set aside.

2 With a sharp knife, slash the top of each cupcake and push a piece of strawberry into the center. Pipe frosting onto each cupcake and decorate with the red sugar flowers. Serve immediately.

Makes 12

Celebration Cakes

Preparation 12 mins **Cooking** 20 mins **Calories** 27

3 eggs
½ cup butter, softened
1 cup superfine sugar
½ cup milk
1 ½ cups self-rising flour, sifted
1 tsp vanilla extract
½ tsp yellow food coloring
zest of 1 lemon

Topping
1 cup confectioner's sugar
½ cup butter, room temperature
2 drops green food coloring
12 novelty candles (optional)

1 Preheat the oven to 160°C (325°F). Line a 12-cupcake pan with cupcake papers. In a medium-sized bowl, lightly beat the eggs, add butter and sugar, then mix until light and fluffy.

2 Add milk, flour, vanilla, yellow food coloring and zest and stir to combine. Place in a blender and beat for 2 minutes, until light and creamy.

3 Divide the mixture evenly between the cake papers. Bake for 18–20 minutes until risen and firm to touch. Allow to cool for a few minutes and then transfer to a wire rack. Allow to cool fully before frosting.

Topping

1 Meanwhile, combine all the topping ingredients, and mix with a wooden spoon until well combined. Using the back of a teaspoon, apply frosting to each cupcake. Top each cupcake with a novelty candle.

Makes 12

Easter Choc

Preparation 12 mins **Cooking** 20 mins **Calories** 50

3 eggs
½ cup butter, softened
1 cup superfine sugar
½ cup milk
1½ cups self-rising flour, sifted
1 tsp vanilla extract
200g (8oz) bittersweet chocolate pieces
1 tbsp cocoa powder

Topping

100g (4oz) bittersweet chocolate
1 tbsp butter
⅓ cup whipping cream
½ cup butter, room temperature
½ cup confectioner's sugar
36 small easter eggs

1 Preheat the oven to 160°C (325°F). Line a 12-cupcake pan with cupcake papers. In a medium-sized bowl, lightly beat the eggs, add butter and sugar, then mix until light and fluffy.

2 Add milk, flour and vanilla, and stir to combine. Add remaining ingredients. Place in a blender and beat for 2 minutes, until light and creamy.

3 Divide the mixture evenly between the cake papers. Bake for 18–20 minutes until risen and firm to touch. Allow to cool for a few minutes and then transfer to a wire rack. Allow to cool fully before frosting.

Topping

1 Meanwhile, combine the chocolate and tablespoon of butter in a medium-sized saucepan over a medium heat. As the mixture begins to melt, add cream slowly, then reduce heat to low, stirring constantly, until mixture thickens. Remove from heat and cool.

2 Combine butter and confectioner's sugar, mix with a wooden spoon, then beat with the spoon until light and fluffy. Add melted chocolate and combine. Spoon onto cupcakes and place 3 easter eggs on top of each cupcake.

Makes 12

Lamington Tops

Preparation 12 mins **Cooking** 20 mins **Calories** 52

3 eggs
½ cup butter, softened
1 cup superfine sugar
½ cup milk
1½ cups self-rising flour, sifted
1 tsp vanilla extract
1 tbsp cocoa powder

Topping
100g (4oz) bittersweet chocolate
1 tbsp butter
⅓ cup whipping cream
½ cup confectioner's sugar
½ cup butter, room temperature
200g (8oz) flaked coconut

Note: A lamington is an iconic Australian cake named after a Governor of Queensland.

1 Preheat the oven to 160°C (325°F). Line a 12-cupcake pan with cupcake papers. In a medium-sized bowl, lightly beat the eggs, add butter and sugar, then mix until light and fluffy.

2 Add milk, flour and vanilla, and stir to combine. Add remaining ingredients. Place in a blender and beat for 2 minutes, until light and creamy.

3 Divide the mixture evenly between the cake papers. Bake for 18–20 minutes until risen and firm to touch. Allow to cool for a few minutes and then transfer to a wire rack. Allow to cool fully before frosting.

Topping

1 Meanwhile, combine the chocolate and tablespoon of butter in a medium-sized saucepan over a medium heat. As the mixture begins to melt, add cream slowly, then reduce heat to low, stirring constantly, until mixture thickens. Remove from heat and cool.

2 Combine butter and confectioner's sugar, mix with a wooden spoon, then beat with the spoon until light and fluffy. Add melted chocolate and combine, and spoon frosting onto cupcakes. Place coconut onto a small plate and roll each cupcake on it to achieve desired effect.

Makes 12

Vanilla Rudolphs

Preparation 12 mins **Cooking** 20 mins **Calories** 60

3 eggs
½ cup butter, softened
1 cup superfine sugar
½ cup milk
1½ cups self-rising flour, sifted
2 tsps vanilla extract

Topping
100g (4oz) bittersweet chocolate
1 tbsp butter
⅓ cup whipping cream
novelty reindeers (available from specialist cake decoration stores)

1 Preheat the oven to 160°C (325°F). Line a 12-cupcake pan with cupcake papers. In a medium-sized bowl, lightly beat the eggs, add butter and sugar, then mix until light and fluffy.

2 Add milk, flour and vanilla, and stir to combine. Place in a blender and beat for 2 minutes, until light and creamy.

3 Divide the mixture evenly between the cake papers. Bake for 18–20 minutes until risen and firm to touch. Allow to cool for a few minutes and then transfer to a wire rack. Allow to cool fully before frosting.

Topping

1 Meanwhile, combine the chocolate and butter in a medium-sized saucepan over a medium heat. As the mixture begins to melt, reduce heat to low, and add cream slowly, stirring constantly until the mixture thickens. Remove from heat and cool. Decorate the top of each cake with a novelty reindeer.

Makes 12

Playtime

Preparation 12 mins **Cooking** 20 mins **Calories** 30

3 eggs
½ cup butter, softened
1 cup superfine sugar
½ cup milk
1½ cups self-rising flour, sifted
1 tsp vanilla extract

Topping
200g (8oz) colored fondant
writing icing

*Variation: letters could
be drawn on top of each
cupcake to spell out your
child's name.*

1 Preheat the oven to 160°C (325°F). Line a
   12-cupcake pan with cupcake papers. In a
   medium-sized bowl, lightly beat the eggs, add
   butter and sugar, then mix until light and fluffy.

2 Add milk, flour and vanilla, and stir to combine.
   Place in a blender and beat for 2 minutes, until
   light and creamy.

3 Divide the mixture evenly between the cake
   papers. Bake for 18–20 minutes until risen and
   firm to touch. Allow to cool for a few minutes
   and then transfer to a wire rack. Allow to cool
   fully before frosting.

Topping

1 Meanwhile, using a rolling pin roll out the
   fondant to 3mm (⅛in) thick. Using a cookie
   cutter or sharp small knife, cut small circles and
   use to top cupcakes. Draw numbers on top with
   the writing icing.

Makes 12

Choc Chic

Preparation 12 mins **Cooking** 20 mins **Calories** 38

3 eggs
½ cup butter, softened
1 cup superfine sugar
½ cup milk
1½ cups self-rising flour, sifted
1 tsp vanilla extract
200g (8oz) bittersweet chocolate pieces
1 tbsp cocoa powder

Topping
100g (4oz) bittersweet chocolate
1 tbsp butter
⅓ cup whipping cream
½ cup confectioner's sugar
1½ cups butter, room temperature
novelty chickens (available from cake decoration shops)

1 Preheat the oven to 160°C (325°F). Line a 12-cupcake pan with cupcake papers. In a medium-sized bowl, lightly beat the eggs, add butter and sugar, then mix until light and fluffy.

2 Add milk, flour and vanilla, and stir to combine. Add remaining ingredients. Place in a blender and beat for 2 minutes, until light and creamy.

3 Divide the mixture evenly between the cake papers. Bake for 18–20 minutes until risen and firm to touch. Allow to cool for a few minutes and then transfer to a wire rack. Allow to cool fully before frosting.

Topping

1 Meanwhile, combine the chocolate and tablespoon of butter in a medium-sized saucepan over a medium heat. As the mixture begins to melt, add cream slowly, and reduce heat to low, stirring constantly, until mixture thickens. Remove from heat and cool.

2 Combine butter and confectioner's sugar, mix with a wooden spoon, then beat with the spoon until light and fluffy. Add melted chocolate, combine, and spoon onto cupcakes. Add novelty chickens to the top of each cupcake.

Makes 12

Chai Chai

Preparation 12 mins **Cooking** 25 mins **Calories** 27

¼ cup chai mixture (Indian spiced tea)

¼ cup hot water

3 eggs

½ cup butter, softened

1 cup superfine sugar

¼ cup milk

1½ cups self-rising flour, sifted

1 tsp vanilla extract

1 tsp cinnamon

1 tsp nutmeg

Topping

¼ cup brown sugar

2 tbsps warm water

cinnamon sugar

12 star anise

1 Preheat the oven to 160°C (325°F). Line a 12 cupcake pan with cup cake papers.

2 In a small bowl, add hot water to the spiced tea mixture, stand for 15 minutes, strain and set aside. In a medium-sized bowl, lightly beat the eggs, add butter and sugar, then mix until light and fluffy.

3 Add milk and flour, and stir to combine. Add remaining ingredients. Place in a blender and beat for 2 minutes, until light and creamy. Add chai tea to mix and stir through.

4 Divide the mixture evenly between the cake papers. Bake for 18–20 minutes until risen and firm to touch. Allow to cool for a few minutes and then transfer to a wire rack. Allow to cool fully before frosting.

Topping

1 Meanwhile, combine the raw sugar and water in a small bowl, mix with a wooden spoon, spoon onto cupcakes and sprinkle with cinnamon sugar. Decorate each cupcake with a single star anise.

Makes 12

Sticky Date

Preparation 12 mins **Cooking** 20 mins **Calories** 27

2 eggs

¾ cup butter, room temperature

¾ cup superfine sugar

1 cup self-rising flour, sifted

¾ cup water

400g (14oz) dates, chopped

2 tsps instant coffee powder

1 tsp baking soda

1 tsp vanilla extract

1 cup ground almond flour

½ cup walnuts, finely chopped

Topping

1 cup packed light brown sugar

⅓ cup sweet butter

2 tbsp water

1 tsp vanilla extract

50g (2oz) dates

1 Preheat the oven to 160°C (325°F). Line a 12-cupcake pan with cupcake papers. In a medium-sized bowl, lightly beat the eggs, add butter and sugar, then mix until light and fluffy.

2 Add water and flour, and stir to combine. Add remaining ingredients. Mix with a wooden spoon for 2 minutes, until light and creamy.

3 Divide the mixture evenly between the cake papers. Bake for 18–20 minutes until risen and firm to touch. Allow to cool for a few minutes and then transfer to a wire rack. Allow to cool fully before frosting.

Topping

1 Meanwhile, combine sugar, butter, water and vanilla in a saucepan. Bring to a simmer over medium-low heat, stirring constantly. Without stirring again, simmer for 1 minute. Remove from heat, allow to cool and spoon onto cakes. Top each cupcake with a date and more sugar mixture. Heat the top of each cupcake with a blowtorch, being careful not to scorch the paper or the dates.

Makes 12

Caramel Nougat

Preparation 12 mins **Cooking** 20 mins **Calories** 27

3 eggs
½ cup butter, softened
1 cup superfine sugar
½ cup milk
1½ cups self-rising flour
1 tsp vanilla extract

Topping
1 cup confectioner's sugar
½ cup butter, room
temperature
100g (4oz) nougat

1 Preheat the oven to 160°C (325°F). Line a 12-cupcake pan with cupcake papers. In a medium-sized bowl, lightly beat the eggs, add butter and sugar, then mix until light and fluffy.

2 Add milk, flour and vanilla, and stir to combine. Place in a blender and beat for 2 minutes, until light and creamy.

3 Divide the mixture evenly between the cake papers. Bake for 18–20 minutes until risen and firm to touch. Allow to cool for a few minutes and then transfer to a wire rack. Allow to cool fully before frosting.

Topping

1 Meanwhile, combine confectioner's sugar and butter in a small bowl, mix, and add chopped nougat. Stir and spoon onto cupcakes in mounds.

Makes 12

Pistachio Zinger

Preparation 12 mins **Cooking** 20 mins **Calories** 40

3 eggs
½ cup butter, softened
1 cup superfine sugar
½ cup yogurt
2 cups self-rising flour, sifted
1 tsp vanilla extract
1 zucchini, grated
juice of ½ a lime
zest of 1 lime
½ cup pistachio nuts

Topping
1 cup confectioner's sugar
½ cup butter, room temperature
zest of 1 lime
½ cup pistachio nuts

1 Preheat the oven to 160°C (325°F). Line a 12-cupcake pan with cupcake papers. In a medium-sized bowl, lightly beat the eggs, add butter and sugar, then mix until light and fluffy.

2 Add yogurt, flour and vanilla, and stir to combine. Place in a blender and beat for 2 minutes, until light and creamy. Add zucchini, lime juice, zest and pistachio nuts and mix through.

3 Divide the mixture evenly between the cake papers. Bake for 18–20 minutes until risen and firm to touch. Allow to cool for a few minutes and then transfer to a wire rack. Allow to cool fully before frosting.

Topping

1 Meanwhile, combine half the confectioner's sugar and butter, mix with a wooden spoon, then add remaining confectioner's sugar and butter, and beat with the spoon until light and fluffy. Add lime zest and half of the pistachios and mix through.

2 Apply frosting to cupcakes with the back of a spoon or a small spatula, and sprinkle each cake with a few of the remaining nuts.

Makes 12

Hazelnut Express

Preparation 12 mins **Cooking** 20 mins **Calories** 42

3 eggs
½ cup butter, softened
1 cup superfine sugar
½ cup milk
1 cup self-rising flour, sifted
⅓ tsp baking powder
½ cup hazelnut meal
½ cup hazelnuts, chopped
¼ cup cocoa powder
2 tbsps instant coffee powder

Topping
1 cup confectioner's sugar
½ cup unsalted butter
1 tbsp hazelnut liqueur
12 coffee beans

1 Preheat the oven to 160°C (325°F). Line a 12-cupcake pan with cupcake papers. In a medium-sized bowl, lightly beat the eggs, add butter and sugar, then mix until light and fluffy.

2 Add milk and flour, and stir to combine. Add remaining cake ingredients. Mix with a wooden spoon for 2 minutes, until light and creamy.

3 Divide the mixture evenly between the cake papers. Bake for 18–20 minutes until risen and firm to touch. Allow to cool for a few minutes and then transfer to a wire rack. Allow to cool fully before frosting.

Topping

1 Meanwhile, combine all topping ingredients except for coffee beans in a small bowl, mix with wooden spoon, and spoon onto cupcakes. Decorate each cake with a coffee bean.

Makes 12

Marmalade Pecan

Preparation 12 mins **Cooking** 20 mins **Calories** 30

3 eggs
½ cup butter, softened
1 cup superfine sugar
¼ cup milk
1½ cups self-rising flour, sifted
½ tsp cocoa powder
zest of 1 small orange
juice of 1 small orange
¼ cup pecans, chopped

Topping
1 cup confectioner's sugar
½ cup butter, room temperature
¼ cup orange juice
2 tbsps marmalade
12 pecan pieces

1 Preheat the oven to 160°C (325°F). Line a 12-cupcake pan with cupcake papers. In a medium-sized bowl, lightly beat the eggs, add butter and sugar, then mix until light and fluffy.

2 Add milk, flour and cocoa powder, and stir to combine. Place in a blender and beat for 2 minutes, until light and creamy. Add zest, juice and nuts, and stir.

3 Divide the mixture evenly between the cake papers. Bake for 18–20 minutes until risen and firm to touch. Allow to cool for a few minutes and then transfer to a wire rack. Allow to cool fully before frosting.

Topping

1 Meanwhile, combine confectioner's sugar, butter and orange juice into a bowl; beat with a whisk until light and fluffy. Combine with marmalade. Spoon glaze over the cupcakes and top with a pecan piece.

Makes 12

Index